PRESIDENTIAL LIBRARIES™

FRANKLIN D. ROOSEVELT
LIBRARY AND MUSEUM

Amy Margaret

The Rosen Publishing Group's

PowerKids Press™

New York

For my Aunt Jane

Acknowledgement: The author would like to thank Lynn A. Bassanese, Director of Public Programs at the FDR Library and Museum, for her invaluable assistance on this project.

Published in 2004 by The Rosen Publishing Group, Inc.
29 East 21st Street, New York, NY 10010

First Edition

Editor: Joanne Riethoff
Book Design: Maria E. Melendez

Photo credits: Cover, title page, pp. 6, 8, 9, 10, 12, 16, 17 (bottom), 19 (top), 20, 21 courtesy Franklin D. Roosevelt Library; pp. 4, 5, 7 (top), 11, 17 (top), 22 Cindy Reiman; p. 7 (bottom) Lynn A. Bassanese; p. 13 Still Picture Branch, National Archives and Records Administration; p. 14 © AP Wide World; p. 15 © Bettmann Archive/CORBIS; pp. 18, 19 (bottom) courtesy Franklin D. Roosevelt Library/Margaret Suckley.

Margaret, Amy.
Franklin D. Roosevelt Library and Museum / Amy Margaret.— 1st ed.
    p. cm. — (The presidential libraries)
Includes bibliographical references and index.
ISBN 0-8239-6268-7 (library binding)
1. Franklin D. Roosevelt Library—Juvenile literature. 2. Roosevelt, Franklin D. (Franklin Delano), 1882–1945—Archives—Juvenile literature. 3. Presidents—United States—Archives—Juvenile literature. 4. Roosevelt, Franklin D. (Franklin Delano), 1882–1945—Museums—New York (State)—Hyde Park—Juvenile literature. 5. Roosevelt, Franklin D. (Franklin Delano), 1882–1945—Juvenile literature. 6. Presidents—United States—Biography—Juvenile literature. [1. Franklin D. Roosevelt Library. 2. Roosevelt, Franklin D. (Franklin Delano), 1882–1945. 3. Presidents.] I. Title.
E742.5.R69 M37 2003

2001006669

Manufactured in the United States of America

CONTENTS

THE PRESIDENTIAL LIBRARY

There are 10 official presidential libraries in the United States. A presidential library holds papers and historical materials from a specific president's time in office. When a president leaves office, the National Archives and Records Administration (NARA) gets this material. The library also contains displays about that president.

Franklin Delano Roosevelt, or FDR, was the president of the United States from 1933 to 1945. He was the first to organize a presidential library. During his second term in the White House, FDR thought all presidential materials should be available to the public. These materials include personal letters, memos written during all of FDR's positions in various **political** offices, and papers from different political groups. These were gathered for the presidential library. Until 1978, records created by either the president or his staff were the president's property. The Presidential Records Act of 1978 made these documents belong to the U.S. government.

More than 130,000 people visit the FDR Library and Museum (below) each year. Both FDR's and his wife Eleanor's papers are held in the FDR Library and Museum. Outside the library and museum entrance is a statue of FDR's head and shoulders (right). It was sculpted by a man named Walter Russell.

THE WAR PRESIDENT

FRANKLIN DELANO ROOSEVELT

PRESIDENT
OF THE
UNITED STATES
1932 – 1945

FDR'S LIBRARY

Construction of the FDR Library and Museum began in 1939 in Roosevelt's hometown, Hyde Park, New York, next to the house in which he grew up. FDR **donated** this land for the library. The library and the museum were built using money from private donations. They are in the same building, with the library on the second floor and the museum on the first floor. On June 30, 1941, the FDR Library and Museum opened to visitors.

The National Archives and Records Administration (NARA) takes care of the 10 presidential libraries. Thousands of visitors and researchers visit the libraries every year to learn about each president and his time in office.

FDR was educated mostly at home by private tutors and his parents, James and Sara Roosevelt. This picture of Sara (above) is shown in The First Fifty Years display at the museum.

At the FDR Museum and Library, you can see the desk that FDR used while in the White House (right). If you look carefully at the items on the desk, you'll see his telephone, several clocks, a few books, and many figures. Some of these figures are donkeys. This is because the donkey is the symbol for FDR's political party, the Democratic party.

FRANKLIN AS A CHILD

Franklin was the only child of rich parents. His father, James, was the vice president of a company that owned railroads and coal mines. Franklin's mother, Sara, was a member of the wealthy Delano family.

Franklin had several childhood hobbies that he enjoyed for the rest of his life. He began collecting stamps at age nine. He collected books on all sorts of subjects. Franklin also practiced taxidermy, or stuffing dead animals so they will look like they are alive. Franklin learned taxidermy by working on his bird collection, which has more than 300 **species**. All of these collections can be seen in the FDR Library today.

FDR's mother, Sara, can trace her family to 1621, to the Massachusetts Bay Colony. Her father made his fortune as a captain of merchant ships, which means he would buy and sell goods for profit. FDR's mother is shown above with a three-month-old FDR. This picture was taken in 1882.

FDR continued many of his boyhood hobbies as an adult. This picture shows FDR working on a ship model. Building these models was one of the ways that he liked to pass the time. This picture was taken in 1930.

FDR also passed along some of his interests to his son, Elliott. Here FDR is working on a ship model with Elliott. This picture was taken in 1912, on Campobello Island, New Brunswick, which is in Canada.

These men are waiting in line for a free meal at a soup kitchen in Washington, D.C. In October 1929, the U.S. stock market fell, causing thousands of people to lose their money and their jobs. This was the beginning of the Great Depression.

FDR entered Harvard University in 1900. After graduation in 1903, he attended law school at Columbia University in New York. He went into politics in 1907. He was elected to the New York state **senate** in 1910. In 1913, President Woodrow Wilson asked FDR to be assistant secretary of the navy. In 1928, FDR ran for and became the **governor** of New York.

In 1921, FDR's life changed forever. He got **polio**, an illness that can cause **paralysis**. Today **vaccines** are given to prevent it. For the rest of his life, he used either a wheelchair or leg braces. Although FDR faced physical problems, he continued his career in politics.

When visitors first enter the FDR Library and Museum, they see a display called The First Fifty Years (right). This exhibit covers FDR's life from childhood through his term as governor of New York.

FDR AND HIS NEW DEAL

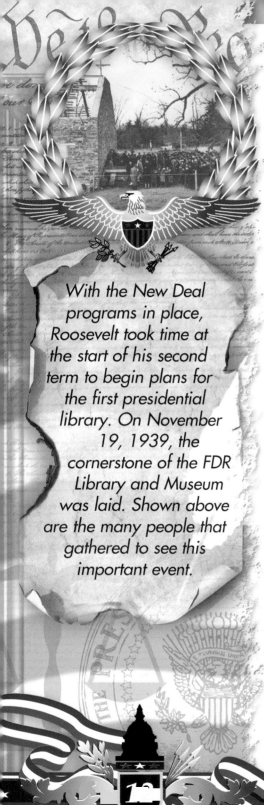

With the New Deal programs in place, Roosevelt took time at the start of his second term to begin plans for the first presidential library. On November 19, 1939, the cornerstone of the FDR Library and Museum was laid. Shown above are the many people that gathered to see this important event.

FDR ran for president of the United States in 1932, and he beat then-president Herbert Hoover. The country was in the **Great Depression**, a period in U.S. history when many people were out of work. You can see pictures in the FDR Library and Museum that were taken during this time.

FDR played a big part in rebuilding the nation. He set up programs to get farms and people working. These programs were called the New Deal.

One of the first programs was the Civilian Conservation Corps (CCC). It created jobs for 300,000 Americans. One of the jobs in the CCC was planting trees across the United States.

The farming industry had been in a depression throughout most of the 1920s. To help farmers, Roosevelt created the Agricultural Adjustment Administration (AAA). In this program, the government would pay farmers to work less. Farmers are shown here (top) waiting in line for their checks in Coosa Valley, Alabama, in June 1941. The AAA would also give supplies to ranchers when needed. Rancher J. C. Duncan used lime on his fields (bottom) where his sheep graze. This picture was taken in April 1941, in South Carolina.

THE FIRST LADY

Eleanor Roosevelt volunteered her time to help people. She is shown above serving soup in New York during the Great Depression. This picture was taken on December 1, 1932. During World War I, she was a volunteer with the American Red Cross. Eleanor Roosevelt turned the role of First Lady into a career.

Eleanor Roosevelt was born in 1884 and was President Theodore Roosevelt's niece. Eleanor and Franklin were distant cousins and met when they were children.

FDR and Eleanor married in 1905. They had six children. One child died in infancy from **influenza**. The others were named Anna, James, Elliott, Franklin Jr., and John.

Eleanor **volunteered** in the American Red Cross and supported women's rights. She even wrote a weekly newspaper column called "My Day." After FDR died in 1945, she became the **chairperson** of the United Nations Commission on Human Rights.

Eleanor Roosevelt supported many women's causes. Here she is shown speaking to women from 20 different women's organizations on October 24, 1932, in New York City.

Eleanor is shown here working with children on August 4, 1933, in Poughkeepsie, New York. She first started volunteering with children in New York City in 1903.

FDR AND WORLD WAR II

FDR began his third term as president in January 1941. Across the ocean, Germany and its **Axis powers** were fighting against England and the **Allied nations**. FDR passed the Lend-Lease Act to try to keep the United States out of the war. This allowed the Allied nations to borrow U.S. planes, tanks, and guns.

On December 7, 1941, Japan bombed Pearl Harbor in Honolulu, Hawaii. The United States was forced into the war against the Axis powers.

The events of World War II are **exhibited** at the museum. The exhibit includes a setup of the top-secret **communications** center in the White House, called the Map Room.

With the whole country working toward a war victory, the nation pulled out of the depression. This picture shows FDR touring a place where women worked to make military supplies and equipment. This factory is in Milwaukee, Wisconsin, and the picture was taken on September 9, 1942. The men were out fighting the war, so women worked in these factories.

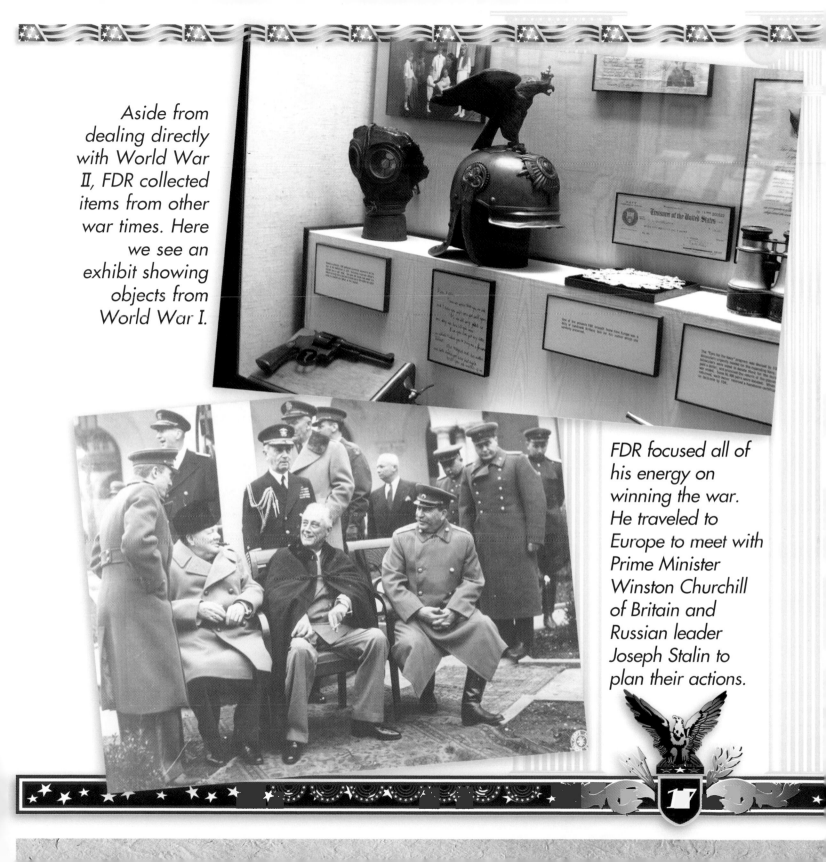

Aside from dealing directly with World War II, FDR collected items from other war times. Here we see an exhibit showing objects from World War I.

FDR focused all of his energy on winning the war. He traveled to Europe to meet with Prime Minister Winston Churchill of Britain and Russian leader Joseph Stalin to plan their actions.

LATER YEARS

The exhausted president and his wife worked side by side during World War II. FDR was wheelchair bound, so Eleanor acted as his legs. She traveled around the states and around the world, dealing with the American people and reaching out to American soldiers who were fighting in other countries. By 1944, FDR and the leaders of the Allied forces could see an end to the war.

Unfortunately FDR never personally saw the Allied victory. On April 12, 1945, FDR died of a brain **hemorrhage**. He died at his cottage in Warm Springs, Georgia. Although FDR never saw it's opening, the museum opened to the public one year later.

In 1921, FDR got polio and never moved without leg braces or a wheelchair again. Most pictures of FDR show him from the waist up, and you cannot see these aids, so not many people knew how serious his condition was. FDR is shown above in his wheelchair with his dog, Fala, and Ruthie Bie, the granddaughter of the caretakers at Hyde Park. This picture was taken in February 1941 at Hyde Park, New York.

FDR had a cottage in Warm Springs, Georgia. He liked to go there to relax. Here FDR is fishing from a canoe in Warm Springs. This picture was taken in 1925.

FDR didn't always fish in Warm Springs, he had work to do, too. Here we see him working by the fireplace in Warm Springs, in 1945.

FDR LIBRARY PAPERS

The FDR Library research room opened in May 1946. It contains more than 17 million pages of personal and presidential letters and documents written or received by members of the Roosevelt and the Delano families, political friends, and others.

There are 44,000 books in the library, one-third of which are FDR's personal collection. The library also has an **audiovisual** section covering FDR's life. It contains 130,000 photos, 700 reels of film, and 4,000 sound recordings. All of these are available to researchers. More than 500 books and thousands of articles have been written using these materials.

FDR had been elected to four terms in the presidency. No other president had served more than two terms. After his death, the government passed a law that limited U.S. presidents to a maximum of two terms. The picture above was taken just before his first term as president. FDR is in his study in Hyde Park on January 7, 1933. He took office on March 4, 1933.

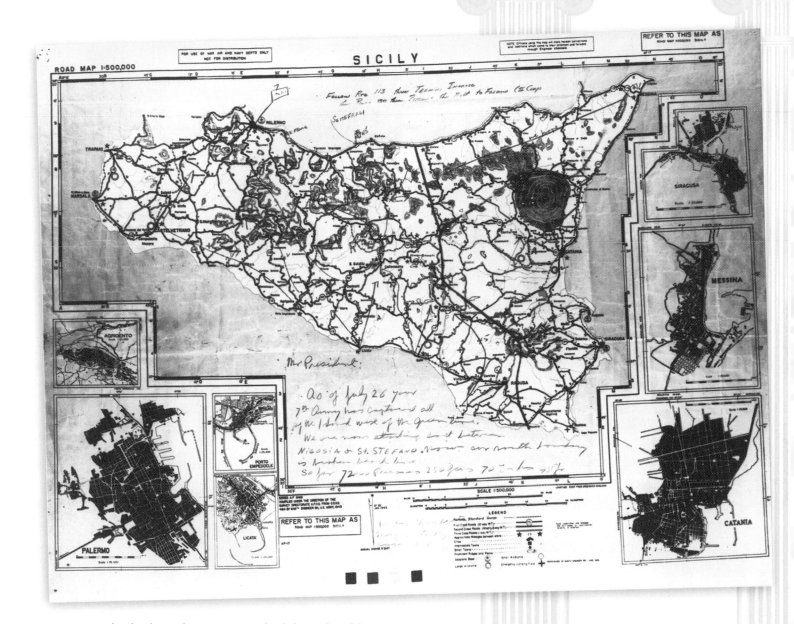

Included in the papers held at the library is a letter to FDR from Albert Einstein, a famous scientist, and this map used by General George Patton in World War II.

EXHIBITS AT THE FDR MUSEUM

When entering the museum, you'll see the desk that President Roosevelt used in the White House. Another exhibit shows the president's car, a 1936 Ford Phaeton. It was designed so FDR could drive the car completely with his hands.

First Lady Eleanor Roosevelt has her own gallery with displays of her many achievements.

Thanks to FDR's presidential library and museum, we can better understand life in the United States under FDR's leadership. We can see FDR's dedication to the American people.

All of FDR's papers, even those that were written when he was a young boy (above), are held at the FDR Library. FDR's personal collections are also on display, including his 150 stamp albums containing more than one million stamps. Also featured are 1,200 prints and paintings of ships and 200 completed ship models.

GLOSSARY

Allied nations (A-lyd NAY-shunz) The countries that fought against the Axis powers in World War II. The Allies were Britain, Canada, China, France, Soviet Union, and the United States.

audiovisual (ah-dee-oh-VIH-zhoo-ul) Having to do with the eyes and the ears.

Axis powers (AK-sis POW-urz) The countries that fought against the Allies in World War II. The Axis powers were Germany, Italy, and Japan.

chairperson (CHAYR-per-sen) A person in charge of a meeting or an event.

communications (kuh-myoo-nih-KAY-shunz) The sharing of information.

donated (DOH-nayt-ed) To have given something away.

exhibited (ig-ZIH-bit-ed) To have been shown.

governor (GUH-vuh-nur) An official elected as head of a state.

Great Depression (GRAYT de-PREH-shun) A time in the 1930s when banks and businesses lost money, causing many people to lose their jobs.

hemorrhage (HEM-rij) Uncontrollable bleeding from blood vessels.

influenza (in-floo-EN-zuh) A sickness that can include fever, upset stomach, and aches and pains; also known as the flu.

paralysis (puh-RA-leh-sis) Loss of feeling or movement in a part of the body.

polio (POH-lee-oh) Shortened for poliomyelitius, a virus that can cause permanent paralysis. A vaccine was proven effective and used throughout the United States in 1961.

political (pul-LIH-tih-kul) Having to do with elections and governments.

senate (SEH-nit) A lawmaking part of the U.S. government.

species (SPEE-sheez) A single kind of plant or animal. All people are one species.

vaccines (vak-SEENZ) Shots that keep a person from getting a particular disease.

volunteered (vah-luhn-TEERD) To have given one's time without receiving payment.

INDEX

PRIMARY SOURCES

Pages 6–10, 12, 16, 17 (bottom),18–21; *Pictures were obtained directly from the Franklin D. Roosevelt Library.* **Pages 4–5, 7, 11, 17 (top), 22;** *Pictures are recent photographs taken at the Franklin D. Roosevelt Library and Museum.* **Page 13;** *Pictures were obtained from the National Archives and Records Administration.*

WEB SITES

To learn more about the Franklin D. Roosevelt and his library and museum, check out these Web sites:
www.fdrlibrary.marist.edu/
www.whitehouse.gov/history/presidents/fr32.html